Acknowledgements
Translated by Jane Sutton.
The publishers would like to thank Michael Chinery
for his help and advice.

A & C Black (Publishers) Limited
35, Bedford Row, London WC1R 4JH
This edition © 1989 A & C Black (Publishers) Limited

First published 1988 Verlag Heinrich Ellermann, München,
with the title, 'Die Blumen-Uhr'
© 1988 Verlag Heinrich Ellermann, München 19

Filmset by August Filmsetting, Haydock, St. Helens
Printed in West Germany

A CIP catalogue record for this book
is available from the British Library.

ISBN 0-7136-3096-5

Flower Calendar

Written and illustrated by Una Jacobs

A & C Black · London

What is a flower?

Everyone knows the difference between a flower and an animal, but did you know that they're the same in lots of ways? Flowers are living things. Like animals, they need food, they grow and they breed. Eventually, they die.

This book will show you how flowers live and grow. Some of the things you know about animals will help you to understand flowers.

For example, tulips have their food stored in bulbs. That's like a hamster (2) making stores of grain. A thistle has prickles to defend itself – just like a hedgehog (8).

Although a plant doesn't have the keen eyesight of the tawny owl (6), it can tell, by the sun, what time of day it is. A plant doesn't go to sleep like this yawning cat (3) but there are certain times when it rests.

Can you see the whitethroat (4) doing a dropping? It's getting rid of the substances that its body doesn't need. Plants keep waste substances in their leaves, and finally get rid of them when the leaves wither and fall off.

Animals move around, but plants stay firmly rooted in the ground. The dandelion in the picture can only move by turning its leaves (10) towards the sun and opening and closing its flowers (11).

The swallow chicks in their nest (5) are going to become full-grown birds like their parents. Plants need to reproduce, too. New dandelion plants will grow from these dandelion seeds (12). Because plants can't move around, they need help from animals. Insects (9) fly from flower to flower, helping them to make seeds.

Unlike animals, plants make their own food. All they need is water from the ground, sunlight and air. They make their food in their leaves, and animals such as this hare (7) may eat the leaves. By producing food for themselves and for animals, plants support all life on Earth.

One thing that plants don't have to do is clean themselves. The mouse you can see here (1) is carefully cleaning its tail, but the leaves of the dandelion plant will be washed clean by the rain.

Flowering in spring

It's still cold and wintery outdoors, but already the flower year has begun. The Christmas rose (2) is out, and the snowdrops (9) on the opposite page are soon flowering too. After the snowdrops, the crocuses (4) open their buds – and then you know that spring is really here.

This male blackbird (3) has just torn up a crocus flower. The yellow colour of the flower is like the bird's beak. Some people think that's the reason for this behaviour: male blackbirds fight each other off their territories in spring, and sometimes they even fight flowers that remind them of birds!

Tulips (1) grow from bulbs which lie deep in the ground. Inside a bulb, tiny leaf and flower buds develop, and food is stored. That's how tulips survive the winter. Now, as the sunshine gets stronger every day and the earth gets warmer, the buds shoot up and unfold.

Tulip bulbs start growing when the soil temperature reaches about 10°C. Snowdrops and crocuses become active at even lower temperatures. That's why they come out earlier than tulips.

After the tulips, it's not long before the soil is warm enough for the other spring flowers to come up as well. Hyacinths (7), daffodils (8), narcissi (6) and primroses (5) start to grow. Suddenly, parks, gardens and window-boxes seem to be filling with colour.

Warm and cold weather, wind and rain, tell plants when to begin growing – but they are also sensitive to the changing length of the day. Longer days and shorter nights are a sign, for flowers, that spring has arrived. Each species has its own time to shoot up and grow. Later, when spring is over and summer is ending, days get shorter again and the air gets colder. All these changes tell the different kinds of plants when it's time for them to grow, flower and produce seeds.

Now let's look more closely at flowers.

9

To you, creeping cinquefoil flowers would look like this.

To a bee, they'd look like this.

Flower heads to attract insects and protect ovules

If you think of a dandelion plant, you probably think of its bright yellow head, which is the flower itself. The flowers are the part of the plant you notice most because they're so colourful and eye-catching. They look and smell attractive so that insects will visit them.

Flower heads come in all shapes and sizes, all colours and smells. Some are dark, some are pale, some look up, some hang down. But although flowers can be so different to look at, nearly all of them are built from the same basic parts. They have two jobs to do: as well as attracting insects, they must protect the developing seeds.

On the outside of a flower, there are usually some green sepals, which protect the bud before it opens. The sepals curl back or fall off once the flower is out. Inside the sepals, are the colourful petals, and inside those are the stamens, which produce pollen. Right in the middle of the flower head there's the pistil, with the stigma at the top.

At the bottom of the pistil, safe in the very centre of the flower head, is the ovary. The ovary eventually becomes a fruit, and the ovules inside become seeds.

Insects are attracted to the bright colours and sweet smells of flowers. In tropical countries, birds and bats are also attracted. At the base of most flowers, there are drops of a sugary liquid, called nectar. Visitors to the flowers feed on this when they arrive.

As an insect forces its way to the nectar, it pushes against the stamens. Pollen is brushed or shaken on to it from the anthers at the tops of the stamens.

Flower petals are sometimes marked with a coloured pattern, to help insects see where they should go. The pattern is called the pollen guide. On cinquefoil petals, the pollen guide is invisible to humans – but in other flowers, you can see it quite clearly. For instance, look at the little yellow circle at the centre of each forget-me-not flower (6).

1	Narcissus	11	Field scabious	21	Lily
2	Apple blossom	12	Garden pansy	22	Lily-of-the-valley
3	Snowdrop	13	Tulip	23	Honeybee
4	Oxeye daisy	14	Red campion	24	Spotted longhorn beetle
5	Hogweed	15	Common poppy	25	Hover-fly
6	Forget-me-not	16	Nasturtium	26	Ladybird
7	Iris	17	French marigold	27	Bumblebee
8	Spreading bellflower	18	Dandelion	28	Cabbage white butterfly
9	Chicory	19	Oxlip		
10	Bugle	20	Lady's mantle		

Stamen
Anther with pollen
Filament
Nectar
Petal
Stigma
Ovule in the ovary
Sepal
Pistil
Flower stalk

11

Sticky dandelion pollen (greatly magnified)
to be carried on an insect's body

Insect pollination

It's summer, and you can hear insects buzzing round the flowers in meadows, parks and gardens. Here's a bee sucking nectar out of a charlock flower (2). Pollen from the flower is sticking to its body. When the bee flies on to another charlock flower, some of this pollen will brush off, and the second flower will be pollinated. Now you can see why flowers, firmly rooted in the ground, need insects to fly to and fro between them.

It's important for a bee to keep visiting one particular kind of flower for a while, because pollen from one flower species can pollinate only flowers of the same species. Bees must be 'flower constant'. You can see that the bee at the top of the picture is being constant to apple blossom (1).

Bees also collect pollen to feed to their young and to other bees in the hive. They carry it on their back legs, held in place by long hairs. Can you see the pollen packed on to the bee's leg, in the picture below?

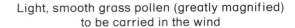

Light, smooth grass pollen (greatly magnified)
to be carried in the wind

Wind pollination

Some flowers are pollinated by the wind, instead of by insects. Wind-pollinated flowers are usually small and dull-looking. They don't have to be colourful or scented – and they don't need nectar, either – because they don't have to attract insects. But these flowers do have to have their pollen in places where it can easily be caught by the wind. They must produce huge amounts of pollen, too, because much of it will be wasted.

Grasses (3) and stinging nettles (2) are wind-pollinated. So is hazel (1). There are always two kinds of hazel flowers on a hazel bush: long, dangling catkins, containing stamens, and little red tufts, which are the stigmas. The catkins are covered in pollen.

On a breezy day, the catkins tremble, and clouds of yellow pollen float down from them. Some of the pollen grains are blown on to the red stigma tufts. The hazel flowers are being pollinated. In autumn, they'll produce nuts.

13

Bees take pollen to feed to their young.

Flowers are pollinated by bees. They can then make seeds and reproduce.

Bees and flowers need each other

What happens to the pollen that a bee has just taken from one poppy to another? You can't see anything happening, because it's all going on inside the pistil. Pollen grains are growing down from the stigma to reach the ovary. When pollen joins up with an ovule in the ovary, fertilisation takes place. The fertilised ovule will become a seed, and the ovary around it will become a fruit.

The poppy's ovary contains lots of ovules, so lots of seeds form. At the end of summer, the ripe seeds are shaken out of the dried poppy head like pepper from a pepperpot.

Poppies need bees for pollination, but the bees need the flowers, too. They collect pollen to feed to their young. Bees also need nectar – to make honey – but poppies don't produce any. Bees visit other flowers to collect nectar.

So bees and flowers need each other. By working together, they help each other. Without bees pollinating flowers, we wouldn't have fruits such as apples and oranges. Without flowers giving nectar to bees, we wouldn't have honey.

Bud

Bee pollinating a poppy

Stigma

Stamens

Seed head

Seeds

14

Summer

Spring

Autumn

Winter

The nasturtium year

In spring, nasturtium seeds sprout.
In summer, new seeds form in the
pollinated and fertilised flowers. In
autumn, the seeds ripen and fall to the
ground. They rest in the soil all winter,
till spring comes round again.

Horse chestnut

Monkshood

Nectar for insects

In early summer, white dead-nettles (1) are flowering along country roadsides. If you find some, you can try nipping off the very end of a flower head and sucking it. You'll be able to taste something sweet. That's the nectar. Insects use their long tongues like drinking straws, to suck up nectar. Different lengths of tongue are best for different shapes of flower.

Honeybees are the best pollinators, but their tongues aren't as long as bumblebees' tongues. Bumblebees' tongues aren't as long as butterflies', which can take nectar from even the deepest flowers. Flies and beetles sip nectar from the more cup-shaped flowers.

A flower mustn't hold too much nectar. If it does, then insects that visit will quickly have had their fill. They won't need to visit any more flowers, and so the flowers won't get pollinated. Bees are good pollinators because they have to visit so many flowers to collect enough pollen and nectar to take back to their nest or hive. Butterflies, flies and beetles only suck nectar to feed themselves.

A flower mustn't hold too little nectar, or it won't be worthwhile for an insect to visit it.

Sometimes the flower displays a special signal, so that insects can tell from far away whether it's worth a visit. Horse chestnut flowers (top left) display a yellow pollen guide when they are young and full of nectar, and a red one when they've been pollinated – and emptied of nectar. The flowers also smell different. Honeybees and bumblebees quickly learn the difference.

There's a thief at work on the monkshood flower in the top right-hand corner of the page. Instead of climbing inside the petals, as it's supposed to do, this bumblebee has bitten a hole through the outside. Now it's sucking nectar without pollinating the flower in return.

Flowers visited mainly by bumblebees

1 White dead-nettle
2 Comfrey
3 Bird's-foot trefoil
4 Red clover

Flowers visited mainly by butterflies and moths

1 Red campion
2 Spear thistle
3 Field scabious
4 Bladder campion

Flowers visited mainly by flies and beetles

1 Meadow buttercup
2 Wild carrot
3 Hogweed

17

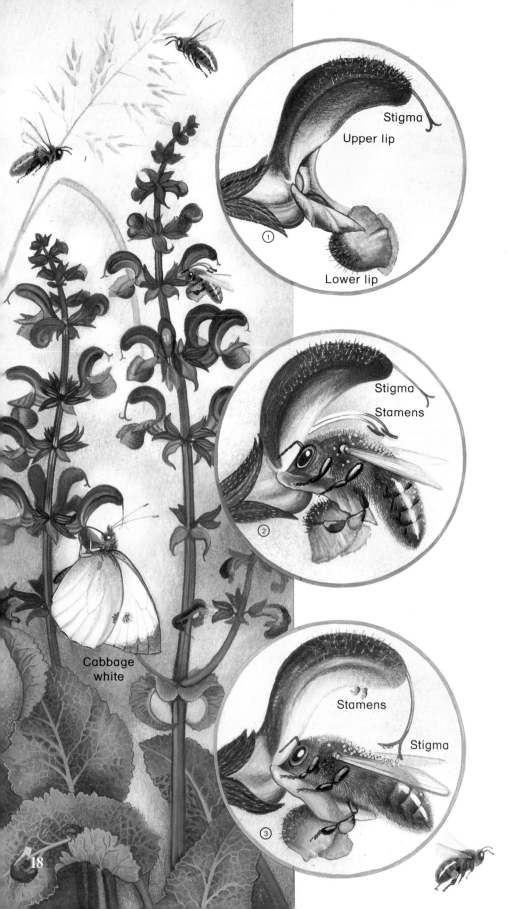

Upper lip

Stigma

Lower lip

①

Stigma

Stamens

②

Cabbage
white

Stamens

Stigma

③

How the meadow sage is pollinated

The pictures on the left show you how meadow sage is pollinated. Usually, bumblebees pollinate sage flowers, but this time it's a honeybee. First of all, the bee lands on the lower lip of a flower. If it's a young flower, recently opened (1) the stamens (which produce the pollen) are hidden inside the upper lip. When the bee pushes its head down to reach the nectar, the stamens are jerked forward. They shake pollen on to the bee's back (2).

You can jerk the stamens forward yourself, by poking a pencil into the flower. The end of the pencil is like a bee's head. When you take it away, the stamens flick back out of sight.

When a meadow sage flower gets older, its stamens wither and its stigma curves downwards. Now the stigma is ready to pick up pollen from the back of a visiting bee (3). When pollen travels from stamens to stigma, pollination is taking place.

Wouldn't it be easier for the pollen of each flower to fall on to that flower's own stigma? Self-pollination does work sometimes, but most flower heads need pollen from a different flower head to produce healthy seeds.

Look at the cabbage white butterfly. You can see that the sage flower wasn't designed for long, thin butterfly tongues. This butterfly is sucking nectar without moving the stamens, so it won't be helping to pollinate the flower.

How the lords-and-ladies is pollinated

A few flowers, such as the lords-and-ladies, work like traps to make sure insects pollinate them. In spring, lord-and-ladies plants grow upright purple spikes, each wrapped in a leaf-like sheath. They let off a terrible stink. Bury-ing beetles and flies – especially small flies called owl midges – are attracted by the smell. They think it's coming from rotting flesh and animal droppings. They expect to find food, and a place to lay their eggs.

But owl midges visiting one of these flowers don't find what they expect. The picture at the bottom of the page shows you what happens. The midges climb down through a ring of stiff hairs, into a chamber at the base of the smelly, purple spike. They can't climb back out, because the walls of the chamber are too smooth and oily. They have become prisoners.

Inside the chamber, the midges eat droplets of nectar, and move about restlessly. Pollen that they have brought in on their bodies now rubs off on to the stigmas – and that means that the flower is being pollinated.

The night after the midges arrive, the stamens inside the chamber open, sprinkling them with new pollen. In the morning, the chamber walls have become less slippery, so that the midges can scramble out. The pollen that they carry away will rub off inside the next lords-and-ladies flower that traps them.

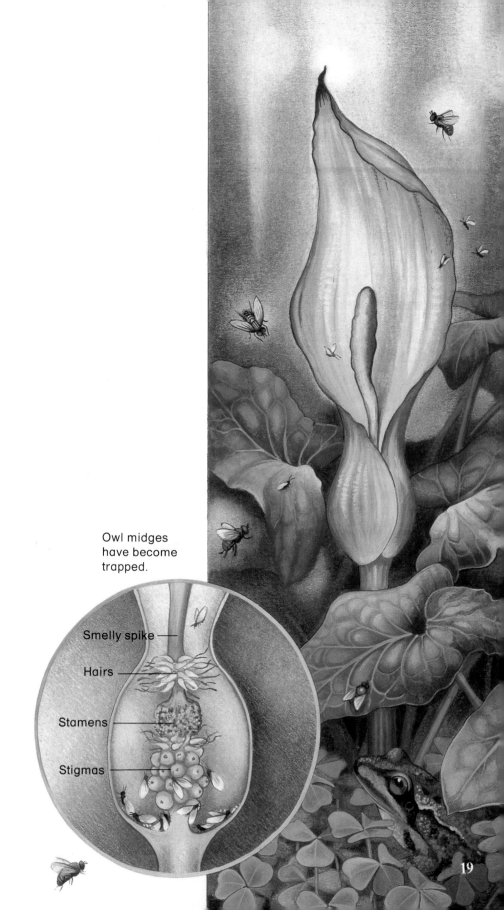

Owl midges have become trapped.

Smelly spike

Hairs

Stamens

Stigmas

19

Plant defences

Deer nibble, cows chew, rabbits munch and squirrels gnaw. What are they all eating? Plants! How can plants keep going, when so many animals take them for their food?

Plants just grow and grow and grow – until finally they die. That's how a meadow stays green, even when cows are grazing on it. And that's why, in summer, you have to mow a garden lawn over and over again. Any leaves that are eaten or cut off must quickly be replaced, because plants need their leaves for making their own food.

Some plants defend themselves against being picked or eaten. If you've ever tried to pick a nettle, you'll know about this already! Nettles sting you with a special acid that comes out of the little hairs on their leaves.

You have to be careful about picking thistles and roses, too. They can stab your fingers with their prickles and thorns.

1 Roe deer
2 Cow
3 Rabbit
4 Red squirrel
5 Hamster
6 Wood mice

Stinging nettle

20

Other plants defend themselves in other ways. Some have sharp little teeth, some have bristles and some have sticky glands. Buttercups contain a bitter-tasting poison in their leaves. Cows and horses won't eat buttercups, and that's why you often see patches of yellow flowers left uneaten in summer meadows.

Do you remember how plants keep waste substances in their leaves? These substances are useful to the plants because they help to make the leaves taste nasty.

Plant defences work well against hungry animals but there's another kind of enemy, more dangerous than these. The enemy is pollution. Humans pollute the air and the soil with poisonous waste gases from their cars, factories and power stations. They even spray poisons deliberately on to fields and roadsides, to kill the wild flowers that live there. Some kinds of flowers have already been completely wiped out, and many others are now rare. We have to make the earth clean, and keep it free from pollution, if we want to save the flowers that grow around us.

7 Song thrush
8 Slug
9 Banded snail
10 Cockchafer
11 Grasshopper
12 Colorado beetle
13 Caterpillars

Dog rose

21

Flower clocks

Flowers open and close their petals, according to the time of day. Each kind only offers nectar and pollen at its own special time, almost as regularly as a clock. It's important that flowers don't all open together. If they did, some would get all the insects and others might never be visited.

As a summer night pales into morning, the dog rose (1) is the first flower to open. Poppies (2) and chicory flowers (3) soon follow – and, later in the morning, bindweed flowers (4), stemless gentians (5), tulips (6) and centaury flowers (7) open, too. The passionflower (8) opens at almost exactly midday.

Butterflies are around particularly when their favourite flowers have a lot of nectar.

13 Humming bird hawkmoth
14 Blue butterfly
15 Cabbage white butterfly

In the afternoon, chicory (3), red campion (9) and bindweed (4) close up again, and water lilies (10) close not long after these. But there are still some flowers yet to open. Evening primroses (11) don't open till evening, and the flower of the cereus cactus (12) – which you might see in somebody's house or greenhouse – actually opens after dark.

When it rains, many flower heads stay closed so that their nectar and pollen don't get watered down. Insects must keep dry, too. They shelter from the rain to stop their delicate wings from being battered or stuck together.

16 Red admiral butterfly
17 Scarce swallowtail butterfly
18 Burnet moth
19 Silver-Y moth
20 Privet hawk moth
21 White ermine moth

Insects inside flowers

Foxgloves (1) are common in woods and gardens. Their long pink flowers look very tempting, but you'd better not touch, because they're poisonous. The spots inside the flowers help to attract insects. Have you noticed the bumblebee inside the flower in the picture? Bumblebees like to shelter in foxglove flowers when it's raining.

Can you see the insect (2) hiding in between the petals of this Gloria Dei rose (3)? It's a rose chafer. It will nibble holes in the petals of the flower and eat some of the pollen.

Tiny beetles and other creatures often make their homes in flower heads. Spiders like nesting in wild carrot (4), when the flowers are dying at the end of the season.

This crab spider (5) has been lying in wait on the daisy (6) to catch any insect that lands there. It can change the colour of its body to match the colour of its background. The honeybee (7) hasn't seen the spider, because the spider's body is the same yellow as the flower. Now it's too late – there's no escape for the bee.

Flower stories

Many kinds of flowers have their own histories. For instance, there's a story behind the plantain (1). This plant began to grow in America after people from Europe first went to settle there. They took the seeds with them by accident, on their clothes and shoes. Plantain quickly spread wherever the settlers went, and so the American Indians called it 'white man's footprint'.

When garden tulips (2) were first grown in Holland, a single bulb could cost a fortune. Everyone wanted the spectacular new flowers. Today, tulips are common, and you can buy them cheaply anywhere.

Some flowers, such as the tiger lily (3), have got their names from things they look like. If you pinch together the sides of a snapdragon flower, the upper and lower petals yawn open like a fierce dragon's mouth.

One kind of flower may have different names in different parts of the country. But it will also have a Latin name, which never changes. When experts talk about flowers, they always use these Latin names.

Campanulaceae
Bell-like flowers

1 Creeping bellflower
2 Spreading bellflower

Compositae
Flower heads composed
of many small flowers

3 Chicory   6 Oxeye daisy
4 Knapweed   7 Dandelion
5 Daisy

Papilionaceae
Flowers like butterflies

8 Sainfoin
9 Red clover
10 Tufted vetch

26

Family names

Can you see the little daisies (5) on the opposite page? They are a species with the Latin name of *Bellis perennis*. Other species, such as the dandelion, are similar to the daisy in some ways. They are relatives, and all members of the Compositae family. This means that each flower head is composed of many smaller flowers, tightly packed together.

Campana is a late Latin word for church bell. Species in the Campanulaceae family have bell-like flowers. Papilio is the Latin for butterfly – so you can guess what the flowers in the Papilionaceae family look like. Flowers in the Umbelliferae family are a bit like little umbrellas.

You could try putting together a flower album. First of all, pick a flower and make a note of when and where you found it. Keep it pressed for several weeks between sheets of blotting paper, with a brick or pile of heavy books on top. When your flower is flat and dry, stick it into a notebook. A book of pressed flowers is called a herbarium.

You can label the flowers in your herbarium, by matching them to pictures in a flower identification book. Look closely at the leaves and stems, as well as the flowers themselves. When you're sure you've got the right picture, copy down the names that the book gives. There'll be a Latin name and an English name.

Meadow buttercup
Ranunculus acris
found 25th July 1988
in a meadow in Dorset

27

Things to make from flowers

Picking flowers in a meadow sounds a nice idea – but wild flowers are too precious to pick a big bunch. Two or three are usually enough for whatever you're planning to use them for. Trim the stems of your flowers and put them in water as soon as possible, so that they stay fresh-looking for longer.

Some wild flowers have become so rare that you mustn't pick any at all. They need as many seeds as they can make, for the species to survive. Other species are more common, and won't suffer if you pick some of the flowers. There's no harm in your gathering a few dandelions, buttercups, daisies, wild carrot flowers or poppies.

There are lots of things you can make with the flowers you've gathered. These pictures may give you some ideas. For instance, have a go at a poppy princess, using sepals (1), petals and a seed pod (2). Then put her to bed on a soft mattress of wild carrot.

If you've got some pressed flowers left over from your herbarium, you could use them for a picture. Arrange the dried petals and leaves on a piece of paper, and then stick them down with tiny dabs of glue. How about making a birthday card like this – or decorating a letter to a friend?

Garden flowers

Now it's autumn – the time to plant pansies in parks, gardens and window-boxes. The pansies you plant have been specially cultivated for their large, colourful petals. But they originally came from wild pansies. How have garden pansies been bred from wild pansies?

Inside each pansy seed there are messages from the parent plants. The messages decide exactly what the new pansy flowers will look like. Every now and then, the messages in a seed get confused, and the flowers that grow from the seed look a bit different from their parents.

Garden pansy
Viola wittrockiana

Wild pansy
Viola tricolor

Many years ago, somebody must have noticed a wild pansy flower that looked bigger and brighter than usual. They must have planted seeds from it, and found that the seeds produced the same, big flowers. The new message had been passed on.

Since then, flower growers have scientifically mixed the messages in pansy seeds. Again and again, only the biggest, healthiest and most beautiful flowers have been allowed to continue to grow and make seeds. That's how so many different varieties of pansy have been developed. All cultivated flowers began as wild flowers, in this way.

There are twenty-five pansy heads on the opposite page, but only two of them look the same. Can you see which two they are?

31

Flowers withering in autumn

Throughout the summer, the sunflower (1) has turned towards the sun. Now, in autumn, its head is bowed down with the weight of ripe seeds. Its petals drop off. Most insects die in autumn, too.

Flowers are dying, but their seeds will grow into new plants next spring. The seeds need to be scattered widely, so that each one has plenty of room to grow. Do you remember how plants used animals and the wind to help them with pollination? Some plants need help with the scattering of their seeds.

Lightweight dandelion seeds (3), are blown away in the wind. Poppy seeds (4) are shaken from the seed head. Ripe touch-me-not fruits (5) actually explode, and catapult their seeds away.

Sunflower seeds are tasty food, so this great tit (2) is flying off with one. But it may well drop the seed, by accident. If it does, then the bird will be planting a sunflower for the spring.

Violet seeds (6) have a separate attachment which is especially tasty for ants. The ants carry the seeds away, eating as they go. The inedible part of each seed is left to grow into a new violet plant. In spring, violets often grow in trails – marking the paths that ants have taken.

Burrs (7) are the fruits of the burdock plant, containing the seeds. They have tiny hooks which catch on to anything that brushes past. Sometimes it's the fur of an animal – or it may be your socks or trousers. The burrs are carried far away, and that's how the species spreads itself.

Seeds lie in the ground all winter. They begin to grow only when the spring sunshine warms the soil.

Flowers in winter

Outdoors, winter brings an end to the flower year, but indoors, you can go on enjoying flowers. You can arrange bunches of dried flowers. Strawflowers (1) are especially good. You have to cut them in early summer, and hang them head-downwards, in a dark, dry place. You can also do this with rose buds (2), geraniums (3) and yarrow (4).

The petals of dried roses and lavender (5) smell almost as lovely as the fresh flowers. You can put them in sealed jars to stop their smells from fading – or you can make lavender bags to hang up in your wardrobe and make your clothes smell nice. The fragrances of rose, lavender, violet and lily-of-the-valley are all used in the soaps and perfumes for sale in shops.

Something else to keep you busy in winter is collecting seeds, such as these nasturtium seeds (6). Plant them when spring comes round again, and then you'll be helping to start off a new flower year.

When you're feeling gloomy in winter, because there aren't any flowers outside, houseplants can cheer you up. Most of them come from distant countries, where the outdoor air is as warm as the air inside our houses. Houseplants need to be carefully watered, and their leaves need to be washed now and then, as they never get rained on in your home.

The Christmas cactus (7) will flower indoors, and so will the amaryllis (10). The poinsettia (8) flowers now, as well; but those aren't white petals that you can see at the top of its stems – they're leaves. These pretend poinsettia flowers are sometimes red instead of white. The real flowers (9) are small and dingy.

Now that you've read this book, you should have lots to think about, all through the flower year. Now you know why flowers look so beautiful and smell so sweet. They aren't like that for our enjoyment. They need to make insects visit them, and it's just lucky for us that they do this with lovely colours and smells.

Contents

Index